ORIGINALLY PUBLISHED IN 1922

OPEN LETTER

The Wanderer starts on its career with this issue, and will occupy, we believe, a class entirely by itself. Its purpose is to present in an entertaining way the real facts about "different" and little-known places and things, both in its editorial matter and in its pictures.

These will always be exceptional. The photographs in this issue, for example, were taken especially for The WANDERER, and are not only exclusive, but are entirely different from any pictures which have heretofore been published. Through the pages of the magazine you will always get the exact truth about a place or a subject, served in an entertaining fashion and illustrated with the finest pictures obtainable.

Eventually we will cover the world. If you have heard of a place about which you have never seen the true facts; if you have heard dimly of certain things; if you know of a place which has always impressed you as being extraordinary; that is what you will find in The WANDERER. In its pages you will see the things that you will never find elsewhere —things which are "catchy" in themselves, and set forth in the catchiest possible manner.

Our aim is to start where others stop.

The first issue of The WANDERER is very slightly premature, as we are allowing ourselves a little extra time in order to perfect our distributing arrangements. There will thus be a somewhat longer space than usual between our first and second numbers, but subsequent issues will follow at regular monthly intervals

A complete story of San Francisco's famous Barbary Coast, with more of our remarkable pictures, will serve to keep our next number from being too quiet.

R. L. GILLESPIE,
Publisher.

The WANDERER

Before the days of prohibition Tijuana was a typical, small Mexican town, sprawling and sleeping in the bright sunlight. Now, as the most convenient wet spot to Southern California, it has awakened to a roaring activity that has entirely changed its complexion. Situated 150 miles south of Los Angeles, and but 17 from San Diego, it is the Mecca for all who wish to cast off restraint and kick up their heels.

LOOK FOR THE SIGN

THE WANDERER

Edward C. Thomas  R. L. Gillespie

Published Monthly by The Wanderer Publishing Company
1012 So. Broadway Place   Los Angeles, Cal.
Subscription $2.50 per year. In Foreign Countries, $3.75.
In Canada, $3.00.

Application made for entry as second class matter at the postoffice at Los Angeles, Cal., under the Act of March 3, 1879.

Copyright, 1922, by The Wanderer Publishing Company.
All photographs made especially for The Wanderer.

TIJUANA
Baja California, Mexico
BY
Edward C. Thomas, Wanderer

Only half a mile from the international border is Old Town, or the original town of Tia Juana, Mexico. As a matter of fact, the Mexicans now call their part "Tijuana," and the old name of Tia Juana ("Aunt Jane") is given to the tiny village on the American side of the line. Tijuana, then, is a settlement of wide, dusty streets and narrow wooden sidewalks—a frontier town where the limit is the sky, and the air is so clear that you can see a long way up.

There are blocks of buildings where every space is occupied by a saloon. Men and women line up indiscriminately at the bars, drink their drinks, smoke their cigarettes, and solemnly discuss the situation in the old-fashioned style. If the men have no companions they are quickly taken in tow by the girls who are employed by some saloon keepers, and who are obstinately and perennially thirsty. Grocery stores and such useless

THE OTHER END OF TOWN

places are conspicuous by their absence, and one somehow gathers the impression that the regular inhabitants must take their nourishment with a sponge. There are no swinging doors. There are no doors of any kind.

Scattered about in the saloons are "money machines" where the reckless traveler may drop anything from a nickel to a half dollar in the slot and after pressing the lever and watching the wheel go 'round, may scoop out the money that rattles down into the cup—provided any rattles down into the cup. If his guess fails to be a good one, he is permitted to drop in another coin and try it again.

It is noticed through the medium of the automobile licenses that Lower California is in Spanish called "Baja California," but the "Baja" is pronounced as if the "J" were an "H." Thus, on going into Mexico, one learns to pronounce it "Baha." Sometimes on coming out one pronounces it "Ha-ha." Easy come; easy go.

The automobiles bearing this strange device seem to know just how to take the bumpy roads of Tijuana, which they negotiate at about forty miles an hour, in spite of chuck holes and large protuberances which reduce other vehicles to a slow walk. Perhaps the educated cars merely hit the high spots.

Close beside the international border is the Monte Carlo—which sounds like a gambling resort—and is. A great barn of a place, the Monte Carlo shelters a dozen roulette tables and other games in proportion—blackjack, craps, chuck luck, wheel of fortune, and any other game which is calculated to give the player more or less of a run for his money.

Crowds of people throng the place, going from table to table if their luck is bad, always looking for their "lucky table." Shirt-sleeved men saunter about the room, overseeing the activities of the dealers. Above the roar of the great room the dealers announce the winning numbers, and the cash registers clang back of the bar that runs along the further wall.

When one is winning, or losing, the long bar is brought into play, on the theory that another little drink wouldn't do any harm. It seems to work equally well either way. Beyond the cafe, in the Blue Room, the player may lose his roll in greater style, but as far as the actual losing goes the barn is just as good.

Just across the road is the race course, with all the accompaniments of the noble art of horse racing. For the trifling sum of $2.50 (which is five pesos in Mexican money) one may indulge his taste in horse flesh to the fullest extent. The strident voice of a woman loudly begs some horse to come on, and the good guessers throng the ring below to collect their bets.

On the outskirts of the village stands the bull ring, where picadors and cuspidors play their usual roles, and the populace sits on the hard boards and watches several gold-braided gentlemen in the act of vehemently throwing the bull. If the spectator protests that the steers are not always as wild and wigorous as might be wished, it may be pertinent to remind him that there is no sense in ruining a perfectly good bull worth forty dollars, if there has been only nineteen dollars taken in at the gate.

At the fight club, situated on the main corner of the town, the crowds are larger, though no one has yet discovered the reason. It may be that people would rather see the pugilists killed than the bulls. Or it may be that those who still have the price may need an excuse for going across the street for a few more drinks.

The universal password in Tijuana is, "How much have you got left?" In other places the pedestrian asks his friend how he is or what he is doing, but in Tijuana he always asks him how much he has left.

It's a great life.

THE MONUMENT AT THE BORDER. SOLID ROCK!

The WANDERER

When the traveler motors into Mexico a grinning official taxes him about twenty cents, and hands him in return a little ticket which says, "Admit One," and which was apparently intended for use in a moving picture theatre. If one displays any curiosity as to the purpose of the payment, he is informed that it is to provide good roads in Tijuana.

After riding over them for twenty seconds one is inclined to agree that the money will be well spent. Tijuana boasts a collection of the worst roads in captivity, and the further one goes the worse they get. The motorist's knees hit his chin, and unless he has a low centre of gravity he fails altogether to stick in the automobile. The minute he enters the country he begins to beg somebody's pardon.

But they have been collecting that road tax for a long, long time, and still the roads get no better.

Many of the saloons have dance floors in the rear or "cafe" section, and here the cash customer may trip the light fantastic toe and other things, with a partner selected from among the young ladies who toil and spin in the various places.

On these dance floors nothing is barred except murder. So skillful have the girls become that they can start a dance in a given spot and finish it in exactly the same place, and still have been in violent movement throughout the performance.

The startled partner is, of course, expected to slip his young lady a negotiable present, and to purchase drinks at what is commonly referred to as the glistening bar.

The WANDERER

A couple were talking dejectedly in a saloon.

"How much have you got left?" asked the woman.

"Four dollars," said her husband. "Not another cent do you get for those money machines."

Two minutes later she was again playing the money machines. Losing what she had, she returned to her husband with a shrug and a grin.

Three young men staggered out of a combination saloon and dance-hall, apparently made dizzy by too much dancing with the girls. The centre one was in a higher state of dejection than the other two, which is probably the reason he was supported on either side by a wavy comrade.

Approaching their automobile, the miserable member of the trio was dumped in the back seat, and the other two prepared to seat themselves in the front; when one, speaking not a word, started back across the street again.

"Hey!" shouted his companion. "Where you goin'?"

"Free drink!" answered the other. "Come on! Spent all our money in that place, so the bartender's got to give us a free drink."

"Good idea!" said the first. "Wait!"

The Sick One in the back seat raised his voice in supplication. "For the love of Mike," he pleaded, "don't go back there! Let's get out of here! I'm sick!"

Without a word the other two young men linked arms and walked solemnly across the street.

Soon they returned, vastly pleased and wiping their mouths. They drove away telling each other what a good sport the bartender was.

The WANDERER

Two Mexicans stood talking on one of the narrow walks. The larger inhaled deeply at one of the dark Mexican cigarettes; apparently he paid no attention to the smoke, as it continually gushed from his mouth as he talked. But the noticeable thing about him was his manner of making gestures. They were so light and airy that they appeared nothing less than dainty, especially in a man of such weight.

Soon he reached for his handkerchief, and it was seen that he wore a heavy belt stuffed with cartridges and an ugly looking revolver under his coat.

A little investigation revealed that his companion was similarly armed, and that, almost without exception, the male residents of Tijuana were ready to do battle at a moment's notice.

Thus does each man carry his own version of the law.

If the resident of Tijuana desires to buy a hat, or deposit some money in a bank, or get something at a department store, or visit the town butcher, he goes to San Diego—that's all.

It simply isn't done in Tijuana. Nationally advertised goods are not kept—even on the top shelf.

A LITTLE FRIENDLY ADVICE

A tired traveler tossed a coin on the bar and attacked his drink with gusto.

The bartender glanced at the money and shoved it back toward its owner.

Continued on page 25

SOME FACTS ABOUT TIJUANA

Departing from the rather bantering tone of this book as a whole, it may be said that Tijuana is a modern, progressive city which is just now introducing many improvements, and which is an orderly, well-governed metropolis in every respect, with its affairs administered by authorities representing both the city and the Federal Government of Mexico. In the local Governor's Palace are found not only the headquarters of the mayor and police force, but federal and justice courts, post office, and other adjuncts of a modern city. Here also are headquarters of the military garrison, which consists of two hundred soldiers, under command of a colonel of the regular army. The government operates the local water works, and is also about to install a complete sewerage system, while the town also has a complete electric light service.

A decree recently issued by President Obregon places a ban on all forms of gambling. A number of offers, including one of $100,000 per month for the exclusive gambling privilege of Tijuana, have been refused—which seems to dispose of the contention that the Mexican Government is in need of money. Only slot machines are permitted in Mexico, and they are heavily taxed. One concessionaire to whom we spoke stated that he alone paid a tax of $125.00 per day for their operation, even though he had but a few of them installed in his place of business. When the Mexican government permitted general gambling some time ago, the revenue derived from this source was used to rebuild the Federal Government Building in Tijuana.

Each saloon, as a matter of fact, pays about $1,000 per month in taxes, and even bartenders are taxed for carrying on their trade. Federal and local taxes on liquor amount to from $30.00 to $40.00 per case of twelve bottles, and bulk goods are subject to an impost of $10.00 to $12.00 per gallon. This applies not only to imported beverages, but also to those which are brought from other parts of Mexico into the northern district of Lower California, which includes Tijuana. Even Mexican beer and Mexican tequila imported into the district are taxed at the same rates.

The management of the race track, in addition to its regular taxes, also agrees to build a school house each year, and to pre-

(Continued on page 24)

THE BIG CURIO STORE—THE OLDEST BUILDING IN TIJUANA. OVER THIRTY YEARS IN BUSINESS, AND STILL GOING STRONG.

BUFFET OF THE "CIA. COMERCIAL DE LA BAJA CALIFORNIA, S. A." (LOWER CALIFORNIA COMMERCIAL CO., INC."). FORMERLY "MIGUEL GONZALEZ," TIJUANA, MEXICO.

FEDERAL BUILDING, TIJUANA, LOWER CALIFORNIA, MEXICO, WHICH WAS BUILT WITH RETURNS FROM GAMBLING CONCESSIONS.

UNCLE SAM'S PROBLEM IS TO KEEP THIS MERCHANDISE IN TIJUANA.

MAIN STREET, TIJUANA

EL HIPODROMO DE TIJUANA

TIJUANA BAR AND CAFE-CABARET

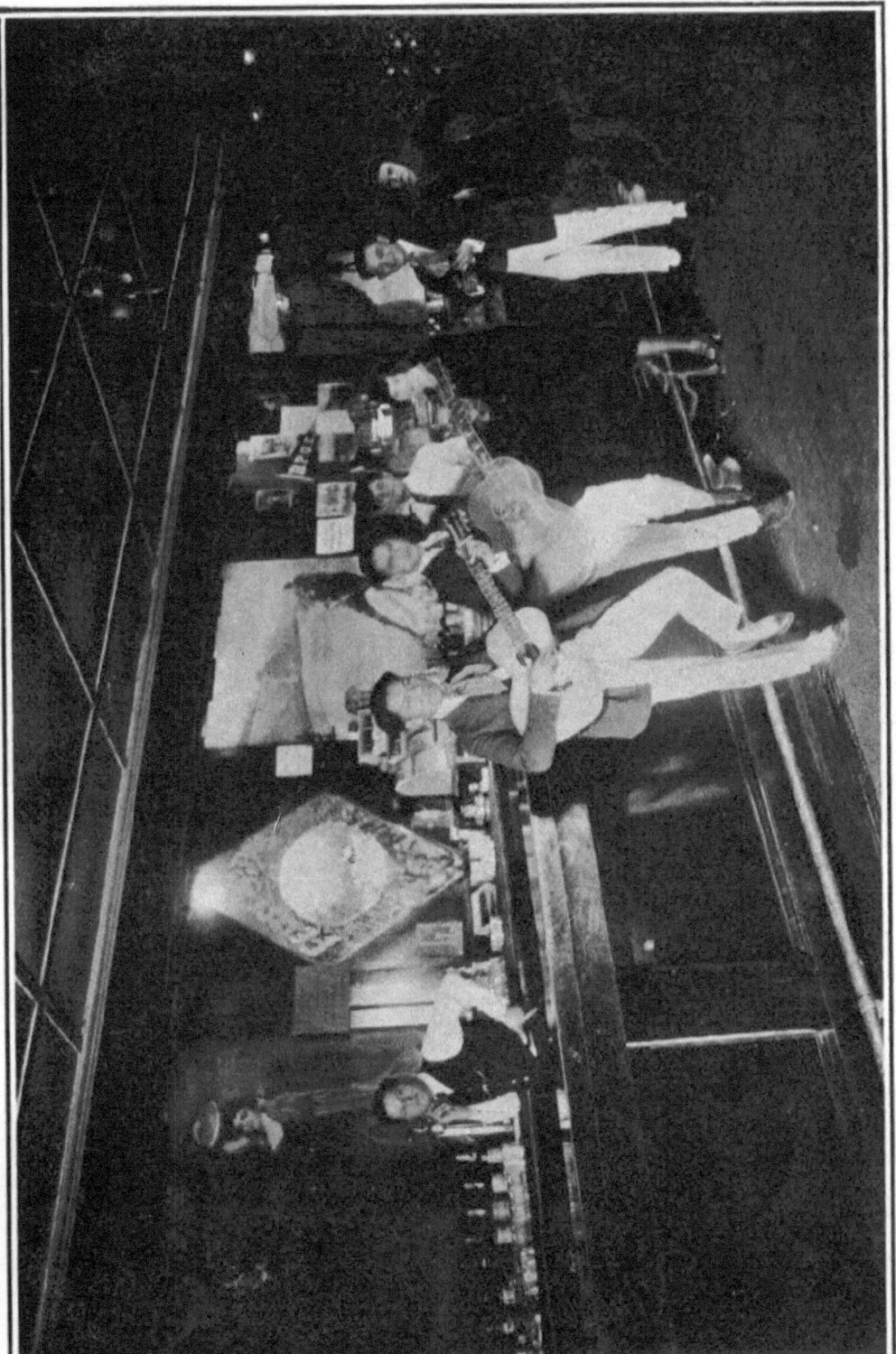

VERNON CLUB BAR, TIJUANA, MEXICO

THE MONTE CARLO. EIGHTY THOUSAND DOLLARS FOR TWENTY DAYS' GAMBLING PRIVILEGE WASN'T SO VERY HIGH. TO THE LEFT—THE "SUNSET INN"

THE SIGNS ABOVE THE CASHIER'S OFFICE, INTERIOR OF THE MONTE CARLO.

THE FORT, ALSO USED AS THE TOWN JAIL.

BOTTLE DEPARTMENT AND WAREHOUSE IN TIJUANA, MEXICO, OF THE "CIA. COMERCIAL DE LA BAJA CALIFORNIA, S. A.," WHICH, TRANSLATED, SIGNIFIES "LOWER CALIFORNIA COMMERCIAL CO., INC." (FORMERLY "MIGUEL GONZALEZ"), A HALF MILLION DOLLAR CONCERN WITH BUSINESS HOUSES IN MEXICALI, TIJUANA, ENSENADA AND TECATE, IN LOWER CALIFORNIA, MEXICO

THE NATIONAL SPORT.

THE "LAST CHANCE"—BUT YOU GO THE OTHER DIRECTION WHEN YOU LEAVE TIJUANA.

The WANDERER

(Continued from page 9)

sent it to the state. The school for the year 1922 is being constructed at Ensenada, and the one for the following year has been allotted to Tijuana. The city already possesses a good school and Catholic church, as well as a residence district in which no concessions are permitted, and in which many highly cultured Mexican families live and prosper. There is a first-class hotel in operation, and stores where all the necessities of life may be purchased. At the meat market, for example, good meats are on sale at prices much below those obtaining in San Diego.

Cement sidewalks will be installed immediately, and about a dozen new buildings are being erected in various parts of the town. The admittance tax has been abolished, and a cement road is being built to take the place of the old one. After this is completed the Tijuana streets will also be paved.

Of particular interest to the motorist is the fact that unexcelled automobile roads are now under construction in Lower California, and a new section is thus being opened up to motor travel. Two magnificent boulevards, to cost $1,000,000 each, are ninety per cent completed, paid for with the money that the government collects from all the concessions. These roads will centre in Tijuana, one leading to Mexicali, the capital, and the other to Ensenada, 75 miles to the south.

A great rise in Tijuana real estate and rental values has been noted. In the principal block on Main Street lots were at first offered at a hundred pesos per month, with few takers. Now they are easily rented at $500 per month, and sell as high as $5,000.

As a matter of fact, the Curio Store proprietors have been offered $1,000 per month rental for their store for saloon purposes, but state that not for any price would they allow the property to be used for this purpose. The curio store has become the centre of Tijuana's tourist activity, with its rare collection of attractive offerings, and as a curio store it seems destined to remain.

This illustrates the prevailing viewpoint of Tijuana's best citizens. Though the saloons are provided for those who wish to patronize them, there are also places like "The Big Curio Store" which are full of interest for the traveler, and which form the basis of the town's attractiveness.

"That coin is no good here," he announced.

"Why, what's the matter with it?" asked the traveler.

"Matter!" repeated the bartender indignantly. "Why, it's Mexican!"

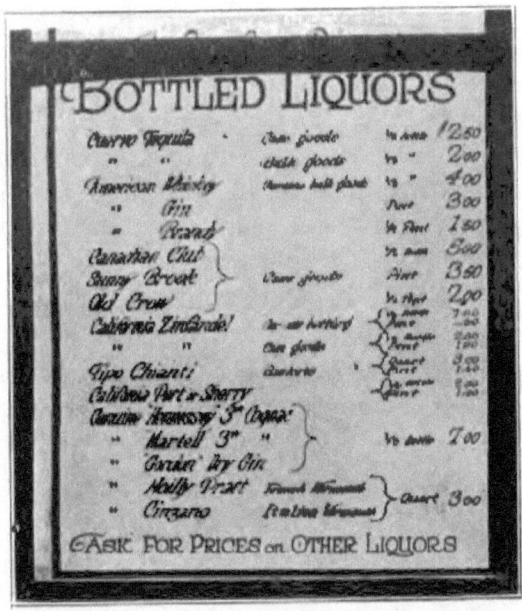

THAT BLACK BORDER IS NOT MOURNING. IT'S JUST THE WINDOW AROUND THE SIGN.

The Governor's Palace, or as it is perhaps more musically called by the Mexicans, El Palacio de Gobernador, is the best building in Tijuana— (as is entirely fitting, when you come to think about it) —and makes all the other show places of the town take inconspicuous seats in the last row.

Not so long ago the old palace burned down, so there was nothing to do but declare a fiesta, and thus raise funds for a new one. For during a fiesta the gambling games are allowed to run, and for this privilege the owners of the games pay a license.

So when the Governor's Palace burned down, the Monte Carlo paid eighty thousand dollars (count 'em) for a fiesta of twenty days, and the other lesser gambling institutions paid less, and the dignity of the government was saved. The new palace arose on the ashes of the old one, and the government at Tijuana still lived.

A little mental arithmetic serves to show that eighty thousand dollars for twenty days means something like four thousand dollars a day, which is a sum not to be sneezed at unless you have hay fever.

Ah, well—

The WANDERER

A touring car rolled up to the custom house at the border, and the customs officials astonished the passengers by asking them to get out, so that they might search the machine. Sure enough, they were rewarded by finding three bottles of what is usually called hootch, concealed beneath the back cushion.

It is a peculiar fact that ordinarily the customs men search only those automobiles which contain contraband liquor, and merely glance in those which are not trying to carry anything except the passengers.

Can it be that the well-known U. S. Government has some secret means of knowing who buys liquor?

At any rate, San Diego garages are full of machines which have been confiscated for smuggling.

A young man stood in animated conversation with one of the girls who worked in a saloon. The obliging bartender passed across their drinks as fast as they could consume them—nay; even faster—at fifty cents per drink.

But apparently they were having no effect on the girl. She always ordered gin, at which the unwinking bartender passed out a gin bottle full of water and a chaser consisting of another

SMUGGLERS, BEWARE!

bit of water. Thus Gertie could drink all day and still retain her value to the "house" and the "boss." With each drink she received a little slip, which she carefully stowed away in the First National Bank.

At length she addressed the bartender. "Hey, Al," she said, "you didn't give me a slip with that last drink."

And in a burst of confidence she said to her new-found friend, "Those are worth twenty cents apiece. I cash 'em in every night."

A large automobile, bearing half a dozen befuddled passengers, had been cruising around the hillsides on the Mexican side of the line for the greater part of an hour, pausing now and then for the purpose of allowing the driver to alight and make solemn investigations. Evidently he was looking for the single road that led out of Mexico and back to San Diego.

At length the car wavered down the barbed-wire fence that separates American territory from Mexican, and came to an uncertain stop alongside an American customs officer, who had been

BIRD'S-EYE VIEW OF LOSERS AND HORSES.

CAMARADAS

sitting on the porch of the custom house that flanks the only gate, and wondering audibly what in thunder that car was up to.

As the automobile stopped again, the passengers straightened up in mild surprise and looked askance at the driver.

Apparently the driver had had enough.

"Say," he shouted in a high, strained voice, "how do you get out of this bloody place?"

"Why," said the customs man, vastly relieved, "you get out right here. But first you'll have to let me search that car of yours."

Two young girls and a young man approached another young fellow who stood in the crowd around one of the roulette tables in the Monte Carlo—two young married couples.

They exchanged grins.

"Dear," said one of the girls, "how much have you got left?"

The player examined the chips in his hand. "Two dollars," he announced.

"Well," said his wife, "we've only got seven cents between the three of us."

In a moment the young husband joined them, empty-handed. "Well," he said, "that cleans me. Let's go home."

As they stumbled out onto the steps the young people giggled.

"Say," said one of the girls, "what shall we do with the seven cents?"

On entering Mexico the traveler must register a description of his car, together with the time of entering, and on coming out of the country must enact a reversal of the process. This makes it a poor place to take stolen automobiles.

But how much more interesting it would be if the regulations provided for registering the amount of money taken into Tijuana, and the amount taken out!

A prosperous-looking individual emerged from one of the Tijuana emporiums, anxiously searching in his pockets. Evidently he had been hard hit.

Finding enough for the customary hot dog, he hurriedly purchased one, and entered into negotiations with the vendor.

"I'm the president of the largest bank in my town in Ohio," he announced. "Will you cash a check for two dollars? I haven't got enough left for fare back to San Diego."

"We never cash checks," said the hot dog man.

The patient banker went all over Tijuana, vainly trying to cash his check for two dollars.

AN AEROPLANE VIEW OF THIRTY-SIX TORPEDO-BOAT DESTROYERS, TIED UP AT THE SANTA FE WHARF IN SAN DIEGO.

The San Diego Destroyer Base.

The man who wrote the song about a life on the ocean wave must have taken a long look at San Diego. There is probably no place on the inhabited globe where there are more venomous little warships than in San Diego Harbor, and they are so thick that they keep them in bunches, like bananas or raisins.

San Diego is the home base for the destroyers attached to the American Pacific Fleet, and the water is dotted with the various divisions of the ships, tied together in units of six, and stretching the entire length of the harbor. There are usually in the neighborhood of a hundred warships somewhere on the premises, and the man who is detailed to keep track of just where each ship is stationed has more trouble than a one-armed paper hanger with a bad case of hives.

The streets of the city are alive with sailors. In fact, one of the principal outdoor sports of the San Diego police force consists of watching carefree sailor boys sailing across prohibited street crossings in rented Fords. If the traffic cop so far forgets himself as to put up his hand, the absent-minded sailor who happens to be driving will step on the low-gear pedal, thinking he is throwing out the clutch—and consequently will continue on his merry way. Sometimes one of these Fords will go for several blocks without an accident.

Tourists who have nothing else to do frequently pass a pleasant afternoon by walking behind an officer and counting the number of sailors he salutes within a given distance. Anybody that says an officer has an easy time of it is crazy. Saluter's arm is much like writer's cramp, but infinitely worse, and officers have been known to duck down alleys and hide in back yards, rather than risk a promenade on the main stem.

AN AEROPLANE VIEW OF U. S. DESTROYERS MANOEUVRING.

I'LL BET YOU KNOW THIS PLACE!

For more than 30 years it has been the show place of Tijuana, and headquarters for all its visitors. Our friends are scattered all over the United States.

No trip to Tijuana is complete without an inspection of our unusual stock. Make this your headquarters.

The only store of its kind in Tijuana!

The Big Curio Store
TIJUANA, MEXICO

CIA. COMERCIAL DE LA BAJA CALIFORNIA, S.A.

(Lower California Commercial Co., Inc.)
Tijuana, Mexico.
Formerly MIGUEL GONZALEZ.

INTERIOR

The Big Curio Store
TIJUANA, MEXICO

with a remarkable collection of
Mexican souvenirs

An unlimited assortment of Post Cards, Zarapes, Indian Pottery, Mexican Sombreros and Baskets, Drawn Work, Carved Leather Goods, and an infinite variety of other curios.

Souvenir Spoons a Specialty

Headquarters for Fine Mexican Cigars and Cigarettes.

Cia. Comercial De La Baja California, S. A.
(Lower California Commercial Co., Inc.)
Formerly MIGUEL GONZALEZ

Reproduced in 2020 by The Press of Ill Repute and ¡Viva Mexico! from the original 1922 publication.

All rights reserved.

ISBN: 978-1-946341-03-7 (print), 978-1-946341-04-4 (digital)

Wholesale order inquiries: chicastj@protonmail.com

Notes Regarding This Tome

This charming tome originally published in 1922 by the Wanderer Pub. Co. is part of a larger series of which this is the first. Despite days of research, I have been unable to locate the title or subject of the second volume. I did find reference to a third volume titled "Hollywood: City of Make Believe" (authored by Edward C Thomas) yet an actual copy of it eludes me.

I have reproduced the pages from the original in their original order save for one change: I elected to move the original publisher's Open Letter from the end of the book to the front of the book and moved the ad for The Big Curio Store that was at the beginning of the book to the end.

While no Wikipedia entry exists for either of the authors, my research indicates that RL Gillespie owned Gillespie's Book Store in Los Angeles, located at one time on 2nd Street (ca. 1911) and later on Spring Street. He also appears as the author/publisher of a street map of Los Angeles, published in the 1930s. Edward C. Thomas has been more elusive and other than his work on the 3rd edition of The Wanderer (referenced above), I have not been able to attribute him to any other books.

Lastly, the reader should be on the lookout for additional titles of interest about Mexico that will be forthcoming in this new ¡Viva Mexico! series from The Press of Ill Repute.

www.ingramcontent.com/pod-product-compliance
Lightning Source LLC
Chambersburg PA
CBHW030142100526
44592CB00011B/1010